THE *Bl*
Y
BUS

John Winterson Richards

Edited by
Thomas Drewry

Colette House
52-55 Piccadilly
London W1J 0DX
United Kingdom

Email: info@bluffers.com
Website: bluffers.com
Twitter: @BluffersGuide

First published 1992
This edition published 2013
Copyright © Bluffer's® 2013

Publisher: Thomas Drewry
Publishing Director: Brooke McDonald

Series Editor: David Allsop
Design and Illustration: Jim Shannon

A CIP Catalogue record for this book
is available from the British Library.

ISBN: 978-1-909365-48-3 (print)
      978-1-909365-49-0 (ePub)
      978-1-909365-50-6 (Kindle)

Bluffing Notes

NEW EDITIONS

Hold your own in any situation with these new and forthcoming Bluffer's Guides®.

BEER
BOND
CARS
CHOCOLATE
CRICKET
DOGS
ETIQUETTE
FOOD
FOOTBALL
GOLF
HIKING
INSIDER HOLLYWOOD
JAZZ
MANAGEMENT

OPERA
POETRY
QUANTUM UNIVERSE
RACES
ROCK MUSIC
RUGBY
SAILING
SEX
SKIING
SURFING
TENNIS
UNIVERSITY
WINE
YOUR OWN BUSINESS

Bluffer's®

BLUFFERS.COM
@BLUFFERSGUIDE

CONTENTS

Where an amateur bluffs only for slight social advantage, the bluffer in business will stake everything – money, home, family, future – on his or her abilities.

THE MISSION

Sooner or later the true bluffer will end up heading his or her own business.

There are two reasons for this:

1. For the compulsive bluffer, your own business is the only game in town. Where an amateur bluffs only for slight social advantage, the bluffer in business will stake everything – money, home, family, future – on his or her abilities.

2. Your own business is the bluffer's home ground. Here, at last, for reasons that will soon be explained, is an activity where the art of bluffing is not merely a useful yet optional extra, but the decisive factor that determines success or failure. Your own business is 99% bluff (opinions differ about what exactly constitutes the other 1%).

The precarious path to running your own successful business is perilous territory, which is where this short guide can offer invaluable help. It sets out to conduct you through the main danger zones encountered in discussions about business, and to equip you with a vocabulary and evasive technique that will minimise your risk of being rumbled as a bluffer, and might even allow you to be accepted as a business owner of rare ability and experience. But it will do more. It will give you the tools to impress legions of marvelling listeners with your knowledge and insight – without anyone discovering that, until you read it, you probably didn't know the difference between a SWOT and a USP.

THE PRO-AM REALITY OF BUSINESS

PROFESSIONAL BUSINESS BLUFFERS

Of course, your own business will inevitably start off small. No bluffer particularly wants to head a small business. He or she would probably prefer to own a big business. Alas, it is a great social injustice that few are able to go straight in at their preferred level. For most, the best way to own a big business is to start with a small one and make it bigger. And the best way of doing that is to convince everyone that the small business is already a big business.

In fact, if a small business is to stand any chance at all, it is not merely desirable but essential that it appears to be what it hopes to become.

The beginning of business wisdom is this: no matter how much people profess to admire them, everyone hates small businesses. This is because:

- Customers feel safer buying from the firms everyone else buys from.

- Suppliers are reluctant to grant easy credit terms to those who are less likely to buy regularly or in bulk.

- Taxmen and other bureaucrats enjoy picking on those who cannot afford the top-division advisers they fear.

- Bankers consider debt-laden governments who regularly default on large loans to be better credit risks than small businesses who miss a single interest payment after years of impeccable financial management.

- Other small businesses resent those who do better than themselves and develop a fine sense of superiority over those who are below them, however slightly.

There is a vicious circle: no one really trusts a small business, so no one gives it a chance, so it remains a small business. To break the circle, everyone must believe that it is:

1. established for longer than it really is;

2. stronger financially than it really is; and

3. bigger than it really is.

THE AMATEUR GAME

The first step in learning to bluff in business is to learn how to spot a bad bluffer. As with most things, there are two reasons for this:

1. Most of the people anyone in business will have to deal with are themselves in business. Although relatively few have studied the art of bluffing, most are experienced enough to realise that their businesses depend on it, and are quite capable of humiliating a would-be professional who underestimates them.

2. It is essential to learn how not to do it. The wise bluffer learns from the mistakes of others.

The amateur has grasped that it is essential to pretend that one's business is more substantial than it actually is. Fortunately for the professional, the amateur always makes the same mistake: the overbluff.

The overbluff is best diagnosed as the condition of trying too hard to impress. Symptoms include:

a) shameless name-dropping;

b) drawing attention to expensive trappings – suit, car, office, etc. (Beware of lines like: 'Sorry, I left my Vertu Diamond smartphone in my Gucci briefcase in the Aston.'); and

c) boasting about successful business deals, however trivial.

The last is the fatal mark of the amateur. Whenever you hear such boasting, you may draw two conclusions:

1. If one makes a big thing out of a little success, it is a sign that such success is rare, and greater success is unknown. Boasting is a tell-tale sign of insecurity.

2. If one boasts whenever one has a success, it follows that the absence of a boast is a clear indication of the absence of success, so a boaster who falls silent, even for a moment, is presumed dead.

Similarly, those who boast about how busy they are only

make it obvious how unusual it is for them. In general, the harder one tries to impress, the more obvious it is that one is desperate.

You should compare the boaster with the real thing, the truly successful entrepreneur. Indeed, before going into business, you would do well to study the manner of those who have achieved what you aspire to.

A successful entrepreneur is so used to hard work, expensive possessions and meeting powerful people that they no longer seem worth talking about. He or she may enjoy so many successes that boasting becomes pointless, even tiresome. In fact, the wealthy entrepreneur will try to avoid attracting gold-diggers and time-wasters (i.e., the taxman

♔

You need to convey not merely that you are successful but that you are successful and modest. The key is subtlety.

and other entrepreneurs) and, being already established, will feel no need to impress anyone for commercial reasons.

Observe this and learn:

a) Never refer to famous people ostentatiously by their first names. The most effective way to name-drop is to use both first name and surname together, especially when talking of someone whose personal name is not generally used, in the middle of a list of more obscure names – made up if necessary – in the same form and delivered in exactly the same tone. It implies you are no more impressed with the great one than you are by other personal acquaintances, or that you know other people who are just as important but whose importance is only appreciated by a select few, including yourself.

b) Don't draw attention to your possessions. Those who are impressed with such things will have made a mental inventory before you can open your mouth, and they will be even more impressed if you appear to take it all for granted.

c) Don't mention business success. If the subject is raised, hint that your successes are too many and too commonplace to be discussed in detail.

You need to convey not merely that you are successful but that you are successful and modest. The key is subtlety.

The bluffer will wish to conform
to the idea held by others of
what a reliable business person in
their chosen field looks like.

THE BASIC ROLE MODELS

The bluffer will not want to look like what he or she actually is, or even wants to be, but rather will wish to conform to the idea held by others of what a reliable business person in their chosen field looks like.

This varies from business to business. For example, someone in a traditional craft who tries to act like a business tycoon is asking to be derided, as does someone in a dynamic service industry who behaves like a country yokel. You should study the norms of your chosen business and ask yourself:

a) Is a premium placed on dynamism or reliability?

b) Does your customer expect you to be aggressive or deferential? Loud or quiet? High-tech or painstaking craftsman?

Don't try to be clever by doing the opposite to everyone else in the same field of business. It can be a useful marketing gimmick, but usually the reason everyone behaves in a certain way is that they have found, over time, that the customer likes it that way.

It is up to you to investigate your chosen field, but most businesses will involve elements from the following basic archetypes:

THE OLD SCHOOL

Distinguishing features:

- Socially secure: never worries about position, power or (apparently) money.

- Impressed by absolutely nothing, and does not wish to impress.

- Impeccably well mannered at all times – not merely polites but show genuine consideration for others.

Advantages:

- So difficult to impress that others will go out of their way to try.

- So obviously unconcerned about money as to be trusted with it by other people. In general, the best way to attract money is to appear not to want it, while the best way not to get something is to show that you really do want it.

- So little need to impress that there is no need to spend a lot of money on expensive trappings – a great boon to the bluffer of limited resources.

Disadvantage:

- Poor imitations are easily spotted. To carry it off successfully, one needs the proper training and practice – ideally a few years at Eton, then one of the more reactionary Oxford colleges, followed by the Guards and/or the Foreign Office.

THE ETERNAL EXECUTIVE

Distinguishing features:

- Talks in jargon, not English. You will have no difficulty in making up jargon. Random groups of letters and numbers are particularly recommended, as few people will be brave enough to admit their ignorance and ask what it all means.

- Takes great pains to appear very, very busy, to the extent of filling in diaries with fictitious appointments, arranging phone calls to interrupt meetings, and turning down any suggested date and time for a meeting to suggest an inconvenient hour instead.

- Obsessed with expensive possessions, especially of the technology kind.

Advantage:

- Easy for the bluffer with a bit of money. One need not be young, upwardly mobile or professional.

Disadvantage:

- It doesn't really get you anywhere; this type has never quite realised how much they are despised by everyone else.

THE FAMILY FIRM

Distinguishing features:

- Appears long-established and places great emphasis on tradition. Basic tasks such as letter writing or bookkeeping are performed in an unusual, even inefficient, way that suggests 'it's the way Grandfather did it so it's good enough for us'.

- Concerned with detail about everything, including quality of craftsmanship and finance. Invoices show comprehensive descriptions of the work done, and the totals are never in round figures but have a few odd pounds and pennies added on to them (not £10,000 but £9,876.53).

- Absolutely classless.

Advantages:

- Creates a marvellous air of reliability.

- Gives an excellent excuse for doing things economically. Family businesses, even the wealthiest, have always looked after their own, and their customers', pennies.

- Appeals to the creative bluffer who enjoys making up his or her own 'traditional' procedures.

Disadvantage:

- Difficult to pull off if you're an orphan or are no longer on speaking terms with your parents or siblings.

THE HONEST CRAFTSMAN

Distinguishing features:

- Looks the part: wears appropriate work clothes and a layer of appropriate dirt (but not the sort that offends), even when not working. People expect it.

- Generally taciturn, except when talking about the job; then likely to talk with enthusiasm and in great detail.

Advantage:

- Customers trust those they can pigeonhole easily, especially if they feel socially superior, and will consider a craftsman who looks the part to be reliable.

Disadvantages:

- Has limited application (though The Honest Professional is similar in many respects, in which case your role model should perhaps be the traditional family solicitor).

- Bluffers may find it hard to stomach pretending to be socially inferior to the customer.

THE ECCENTRIC

Distinguishing features:

- None (by definition).

Advantage:

- In certain businesses, when people see a real eccentric they assume he or she must be very good indeed to act in such a fashion and still survive in business. The information technology sector is a particularly tolerant place for eccentrics, and in some web-related areas it is practically compulsory to be one.

Disadvantage:

- You really do have to be eccentric to get away with it: if you're only slightly odd, people will think you're not quite all there and avoid you. To be acceptable, you have to be constantly outrageous (a 'real character') rather than just awkward.

Whatever model you select, in general you must:

1. Display total confidence and try to appear relaxed at all times.

2. Become familiar with the appropriate technical language.

3. Be unafraid to appear cheap at times. Remember that many millionaires are casual about large amounts but are prepared to haggle over a few pence. Perhaps that's why they are millionaires.

THE BEST-LAID PLANS...

Any business plan will probably be out of date by the time the final draft is typed. However well-researched it may be, it will never actually come to fruition. All the assumptions it makes will inevitably be flawed. The only things that are guaranteed to happen are those that could never be imagined (the First Law of Business Forecasting: always expect the unexpected).

Yet it is absolutely essential that you have an up-to-date business plan. There are two reasons for this:

1. It impresses would-be investors and bankers. The wildest predictions have a reassuring air of certainty about them when translated into business-school jargon, surrounded by columns of figures, laser printed and placed inside a shiny cover.

2. You must be consistent. If separate bluffs are not to contradict, it helps to have one's imaginary empire put down on paper. It also helps to refer to your business plan as often as possible in conversation. If you keep telling people that you're working to a plan,

you might just give the impression that you know what you're doing.

A business plan should have three basic parts, each answering a separate question:

1. the mission statement ('Why am I doing this?');

2. the strategy ('How am I doing this?'); and

3. the financial data ('How much is this going to cost and generate?').

Only the last one really matters but it is important to pad it out with a full plan containing as much surplus information as possible. It is possible, and desirable, to have more than the three basic sections (e.g., human resources policies, Corporate Social Responsibility policy, IT disaster recovery plan, etc.). A business plan must give the impression that every aspect has been thought out in excruciating detail.

THE MISSION STATEMENT

The words 'goals' or 'purpose' are often used instead, and are probably more accurate, but the phrase 'mission statement' conveys a certain sense of destiny. It should make clear:

The business you're in. A short, pithy sentence will do. It should be as broad as possible: a road haulage company should describe itself as being in the 'transport business', a printing company is in 'business services', and so on. It shows one takes it for granted that one is going to expand.

Why you're in it. This may seem obvious – so obvious that people never bother to think about it. In fact, most business people do not go into business with the sole aim of making large amounts of money. Research shows that:

a)   most would make more, certainly more per hour of work, if they were employed by someone else; and

b)   surprisingly, very few who go into business state that their primary motive is to get rich.

People actually go into business for a wide variety of reasons, including: the desire for independence and the ability to make their own decisions; the desire to do particular work or produce a particular product; the desire for a 'quiet' life outside the corporate rat race; or any combination of motives – among them, of course, the desire for financial reward.

It is vital that you sort out in your own mind exactly what you want out of business because that should determine exactly how you operate. For example, an entrepreneur who wishes to get rich will adopt a high-risk strategy more heavily dependent on bluff, but someone who simply wants to earn a living doing work that he or she enjoys will be wise to adopt a low-risk strategy.

THE STRATEGY

A good strategy should be as simple as possible.

Unfortunately, such a strategy would hardly look impressive on paper. It must therefore be expanded with a number of superfluous sub-sections, such as:

Objectives

Not to be confused with 'goals' or 'purpose'. For example, a firm whose purpose is 'to build a global merchandising business' might have as objectives 'to take over the small shop down the road' and 'to increase sales to £120,000 per annum'.

You should be fairly consistent about maintaining your objectives. The thing to avoid at all costs is the reputation of being a gadfly, flitting from one project to the next.

Market profile

This is supposedly based on your 'market research'. However, formal market research is a) expensive and b) useless. The small business is more likely to rely on instinct and personal contacts – but, of course, you cannot actually say that. Instead, this is your chance to state at length what a marvellous business opportunity you have and how the world is crying out for whatever it is you are selling.

Economic profile

This is an optional but wonderful piece of padding in support of the market profile. Just go online and find some recent economic statistics – almost any will do. You can be reasonably confident that no one will check them, but do try to look for something beyond Wikipedia and verify any source that looks a little too good to be true.

Trading profile

This is where you prove your expertise by showing that you know how your chosen business is actually done: standard retail, wholesale, transport, credit arrangements, etc.

Competitor profile

More easy padding. All the relevant information can be found online these days so you no longer need to troll through countless records at Companies House or sift through trade publications to draw your competitive landscape. What you must engage in is a bout of 'mystery shopping'. It involves getting your competitors' sales and marketing material by posing as a potential customer. Everyone does it. Just expect newcomers to do the same to you in a few years when your business is the new yardstick for excellence. After all, imitation is the best form of flattery.

Customer profile

Possibly separated into corporate customers and consumers. The former are fairly easy to describe (in terms of size and business), while the latter can be broken down by age, sex and socio-economic grouping (using the magic letters A/B, C1, C2 and D/E. Don't worry if you are not certain what the divisions represent; hardly anyone else does).

Ad men – the elite of the elite among bluffers – have taken to identifying groups within groups and giving them trendy names. In the USA, for example, the key 'married ABC1 female, age 30-40, with children' demographic has become the 'Soccer Mom', and the 'independent, 65-75' demographic the 'Third Ager'. The self-confident bluffer may well be tempted to make up his or her own. 'We see our target market as 'Ferrets', with valuable secondary markets among 'Gnus' and 'Armadillos'…'

Analysis

Real show-off stuff. There are hundreds of models for use in strategic analysis. Few of them are of any practical use outside business schools – most are too theoretical. You would do well just to hint that analysis has been carried out, without going into any detail. If challenged, invent your own model (ideally something with a university name or a lot of letters in it: the Oxford model or the CGT model).

> In reality, your target market is anyone who pays. But there is a difference between reality and what can be put in a business plan.

If you really must analyse something, use the 'SWOT analysis' (by simply listing the internal Strengths and Weaknesses of your business, and the external Opportunities and Threats it faces in the market); or the 'Benjamin Franklin analysis' (even simpler – list the advantages and the disadvantages of any proposed course of action) – also known, in a slightly different guise, as a 'cost benefit analysis' or CBA.

Target market

In reality, anyone who pays. But, once again, there is a difference between reality and what can be put in a business plan. You should be fairly specific, choosing one of the categories discussed in detail in the customer profile, but keeping your options open by mentioning 'valuable secondary markets'.

Marketing plan

Businesses of all sizes can be divided into two categories: those dependent on large numbers of sales of small value and those dependent on small numbers of sales of larger value. In the former case, there is an established way of contacting customers (such as passing trade for a small shop), while the latter will probably rely on personal contacts.

Since you can hardly say that your marketing plan depends on your 'brother-in-law who is head of purchasing for a major company', you should discuss your 'marketing mix', a useful expression meaning the combination of traditional marketing methods such as advertising, social media, direct sales, mailing and promotions – including 'POS' (point of sale), etc. Even if such methods are entirely inappropriate, they are worth mentioning to show that you are aware of them.

Competitive advantage

Also known as 'USP' (unique selling proposition). Conventional business-school wisdom has it that there are two ways of distinguishing yourself from the competition: 'price differentiation' (being cheaper, or sometimes more expensive) or 'product differentiation' (being better, or at least different). The bluffer's real competitive advantage is of course the ability to bluff, but since that is one of the many truths one cannot actually put in writing, the best USP is probably a nebulous product differentiation like 'superior quality of service'.

Sales forecast
Very important but best avoided because someone might hold you to it. Be vague, or at least qualify it as much as possible ('assuming an increased rate of economic growth', etc.).

Operations plan
A slightly more impressive way of saying 'production plan'. Most people produce something first and worry about selling it afterwards. The far-sighted will secure orders or at least firm interest in their product or service and then 'reverse engineer' a smart way of delivering it, on budget and on time.

Policies
The final touch. Policy, in general, is the framework within which a business operates. The most important policies are the strategic objectives themselves, but even the smallest firm might have a range of additional policies, from major ethical considerations to standard administrative procedures.

A comprehensive list of policies in a business plan would look a little too obvious, but a short note showing that you are aware of the need for them and explaining your procedure for their formulation (e.g., 'Policy will be set by the board on the recommendation of the chief executive.') might be acceptable.

SUMMARY OF THE STRATEGY

A summary of the strategy is an excuse to bring in your real strategy under the guise of a short synopsis.

In general, a good strategy should include:

1. As many figures as possible. Don't worry about their accuracy or relevance; no one will actually read them but they will be reassured to see them there.

2. As many long, American-sounding words and phrases as possible. As a rule, prefix everything with 'long-term', 'short-term' or 'medium-term', and end everything with 'isation'. And never use two syllables where five or six would be more confusing, or one word where three would take more space. Never be afraid of making up your own business expressions: there are so many that no reader will know them all and will be unwilling to state positively that yours are not in general use somewhere.

3. As many repetitions (or at least rephrasings) of your basic points as you can fit in without becoming obvious.

It is a nice touch to number pages, headings, sub-headings, sections, sub-sections, paragraphs and sub-paragraphs using a consistent system. You can then cross-reference ('as discussed in 3.9.14.8' or, in the more archaic style, 'see sub-paragraph 1(4) (c) (ii), in chapter 2, part II, page 37'). This looks good and makes it less likely that it will be read in any detail; only the most dedicated masochist will try checking cross-references. Keep paragraphs short, but make sure there are plenty of them.

Remember that it is unlikely that anyone will read your strategy with any great attention, especially if you make it as long as you can. Anyone who has any real interest in the business plan will home in on the financial data without hesitation. However, it is essential that the strategy that precedes it – and on which the financial data is supposed to be based – looks right to the casual eye.

THE FINANCIAL DATA

This forms the most important part of any business plan because, unlike the rest of it, it will be read. More than that, it will probably be read in great detail by clever people seeking to prove their cleverness by catching you out on some tiny point of detail which could undermine the credibility of the whole plan.

As far as a small business or start-up is concerned, there are four types of financial data:

1. budgets – what you hope will happen;

2. forecasts – what you think will happen;

3. out-turn – what actually does happen; and

4. accounts – what your accountant says happened.

The business plan must include a budget. When it becomes clear that this is completely unrealistic, it can be updated by forecasts which in turn can be replaced by 'revised forecasts' when they, too, prove to be inaccurate.

It is absolutely vital that you are always able to point to an up-to-date plan which shows that the finances are on target (even if that plan was only produced the night before to formalise an existing situation). It gives bankers and investors the reassuring illusion that you are in control.

It might be a good idea to blur the distinction between budget and forecast by using that all-encompassing word 'estimates' to replace both.

The proper format for a budget is a matter of endless debate, but you would do well to forget any idea of trying to draw up model balance sheets and profit-and-loss accounts based on what you think your accountant will draw up at the end of the first year. There are naturally two reasons for this:

1. It is meaningless. Everyone knows that such formal accounts bear little relationship to reality; one would change accountants immediately if they did.

2. It is fiendishly difficult to do. You really need to be an accountant to do it properly, and even then any reader with the slightest training in financial management can, and will, pick holes in it. Even if it is done by an accountant you can never be sure that the reader will not be used to a different system, and if you

yourself were to be examined in detail it could be very awkward indeed.

As with most things, it is best to keep it simple. A cash flow analysis, while frowned on by purists, is:

a) easier to do;

b) more impressive because it involves putting far more figures on the page; and

c) actually rather useful because it shows you how many real pounds and pennies go in and out, rather than how many notional ones.

A cash flow analysis is drafted as follows:

1. Write the 12 months of the year across the top of your page (abbreviate to the first three letters if necessary), starting with the month that begins your financial year, leaving broad spaces on either side for the financial year in the top left-hand corner and the word 'Total' in the top right-hand corner.

2. Down the left-hand side, list all categories of income, then all the categories of expenditure, leaving a line for 'Total' and a space below both, and adding another line at the very bottom – the proverbial 'bottom line' for 'Surplus/(Deficit)', i.e., total income minus total expenditure.

3. Fill in credible sums for each category for each month, then calculate and record in the appropriate columns:

a) the annual total for each category;

b) the total income and expenditure for each month and for the entire year; and

c) the monthly and annual surplus (or deficit).

It is a good idea to have as few categories of income as possible: in business you find that sales you expect, and rely on, never emerge, but money sometimes comes out of the blue from a direction you never envisaged. By not being too specific about sources of income, you will retain a degree of flexibility and not damage your reputation as someone who can predict what will happen to the business. Of course, you always have the option to buy a crystal ball or visit a psychic.

On the other hand, expenditure should be divided into as many categories as you can imagine. The more you have, the greater the number of figures you can stick on a page and the more you can show your mastery of detail. Some will be fairly obvious: cost of sales (e.g., raw materials), rent, rates, gas, electricity, telephone, insurance, etc. However imaginative you may be, inevitably there will be items of expenditure that you miss out. Those who remember interest payments often forget about bank charges and arrangement fees, or put down wages and associated costs (e.g., national insurance) for their employees but not for themselves.

Then there are the so-called 'variable costs' which are supposed to vary according to your level of business but rarely do. These include advertising, publicity and other promotional material; travel and entertainment; and most other marketing costs.

There are also all the minor expenses one never really thinks of in advance but which have to be paid if the business is to operate. For example:

- stationery;

- postage;

- professional fees (accountants, lawyers, etc.);

- company administration (such as the fee paid to Companies House every year);

- office furniture, office fittings, office refreshments (i.e., water, tea and coffee for the troops);

- office equipment; and

- office supplies – the safety-net category of everything from light bulbs, coffee cups, lavatory paper, pencil sharpeners, the office ruler, cleaning and security equipment, and spare keys, to miscellaneous batteries.

Of course, the more categories one has, the greater the chances that at least one will go drastically and noticeably over budget.

Two precautions can be taken against this:

1. Have several categories that are fairly broad and vague so that if one is overspent it will be possible to transfer to another category certain items which could reasonably be found in either: for example, a coffee machine could be classed as office furniture,

office fittings, office equipment, office refreshments or the ubiquitous office supplies.

2. Put a very large sum under 'Contingencies'. You will probably need it. Even if you don't, anyone who knows business will respect your caution and foresight in being prepared.

Despite these precautions, it is still quite probable that your expenditure estimates will prove inaccurate. Expenditure that is substantially below budget can be put down to 'savings due to good management practice'. But so can expenditure that is above that predicted in the budget – such as:

- 'An opportunity arose to buy capital equipment which will drastically reduce our running costs over the next few years.'

- 'We found that employing an extra support staff member will reduce the workload of the existing sales force and enable them to increase their revenues by far more than the cost of the new employee.'

- 'This new marketing initiative will finance itself through increased sales.'

And, best of all:

- 'The public response to our promotion has exceeded all expectation, requiring additional expenditure to enable us to cope with enquiries and increased demand.'

Try to make your estimates as realistic as possible. Make

an effort to think of the thousands of things that might cost money. You won't be able to think of them all, but the more you can predict in advance, the smaller the chance of an unexpected bill cropping up just when you don't want it.

Obtain quotes in advance where possible, as well as information about fixed costs (e.g., standing charges, statutory fees) and put them in your estimates – correct to the nearest pound, not rounded up. It looks very impressive to have a few precise pounds on the page and shows that you have done your research.

The amateur bluffer might try to fool bankers and investors with over-optimistic profits, but such figures always reveal themselves as the hype that they are. It is better to be cautious – to predict modest but acceptable profits while leaving room for a substantial margin of error.

Draw up a first draft on the basis of the most realistic figures you can get and then:

1. Halve your sales forecasts.

2. Double your costs.

3. Double the amount of time your customers take to pay.

This way, any informed reader will realise that you know about business.

PLAYING WITH MODELS

Having drawn up your basic estimates, you might want to play around with them. Using spreadsheets, you can create as many different variations as you want. For example:

More than one 'model' on the basis of different growth forecasts. Using the same format, you can show three different sets of estimates: one optimistic, one pessimistic and one probable – the last being the real one.

Detailed estimates – not only for your first year in business but the next three, or even five, years (although the word 'forecast' should be used to describe estimates beyond the first year to distinguish them from the supposedly firmer figures for that year).

You can either add a fixed percentage to all figures in subsequent years to cover inflation (5% is a good figure as it is best to be pessimistic with inflation and it is an easy figure to work with), or state that all figures are at current-year price. Once again, different models using different growth assumptions can be produced for each year.

The object, of course, is to create a visually impressive wodge of paper covered in figures which should daunt the most compulsive critic. Even with a single year's estimates and no additional models, it may not be possible to fit everything into a single page.

Include a one-page summary on the first page of your estimates and then break it down by notes, i.e., after each category put a number in brackets, the number being that of a subsequent page where that category is broken down into sub-categories using the same format. The sub-categories can, in turn, be broken down by notes for a really thick document. This is an old accountants' trick to increase the thickness of your accounts and the size of their fees.

Finally, the financial data – indeed, the whole business plan – should always be kept up to date through constant reviews in which discredited estimates are replaced.

If, by some miracle, your estimates prove accurate, insert a 'Variance' column which shows the difference, or rather the lack of difference, between estimate and out-turn. Whatever you may be doing at any time, it helps to be able to point to a piece of paper which says you are supposed to be doing it.

STARTING UP

TO BE OR NOT TO BE (INCORPORATED)

There are legal and financial arguments both for and against incorporation as a limited company ('Ltd'). The decisive factor will probably be your tax position.

From a bluffer's point of view, incorporation is desirable because it brings with it two big advantages:

1. a separate legal identity; and

2. limited liability.

If there was any logic in this world, both these features ought to make people more suspicious when doing business with limited companies. Yet it seems that many people – and, strangest of all, many companies – find it reassuring to deal with a limited company.

Perhaps their confidence is based on the statutory regulation of limited companies or on their own ability to check a company's details at Companies House should they so choose. Few do, but it is sensible to conduct a search on any company you are doing a substantial amount of business with, especially if any form of credit is involved. More likely, most people (against all evidence) have a mental image of a 'company' as a large, established, reliable organisation. Those who own small businesses ought to know better, but perhaps they feel obliged to take an exalted view of companies in general in order to protect their own positions.

WHO'S WHO

It is tempting as head of a small business to describe yourself as 'company director' or just 'the director'. But the bluffer ought to have a more specific title to imply being part of a larger organisation, such as 'executive director', 'sales and marketing director' or 'head of operations' etc. You should not hesitate to create a totally bespoke, never heard before title which suits the exact nature of your business.

Some who start out in business give themselves titles like chairman, president, managing director and chief executive officer of their company, and so reveal themselves as people who are unfamiliar with companies. Such megalomania would be very dangerous in a big public limited company ('plc') with suspicious shareholders and keen office politicians fighting each other for every scrap of status.

It is far more effective, and far closer to modern practice,

---

* The ancient and honourable title of secretary ('one responsible for secrets') has been supplanted by the strange designation of personal assistant, which seems to be preferred by the actual practitioners, though there was never any suggestion of the US Personal Assistant of State negotiating with the General Personal Assistant of the Soviet Communist Party in the good old days.

not to have a large number of impressive-sounding posts at the top in order to show a lean, efficient management structure, and for such posts as there are to be filled by different people. There are sound theoretical reasons why the posts of chairman and chief executive should be separate in a big business; in a small or young business there is the added advantage of showing that the company has more than one executive.

It is highly necessary to pretend that you are not, in fact, the top person in the company. This might go against the grain, but there are two definite advantages:

1. Employees have a better reputation than entrepreneurs, who can be perceived as mavericks and therefore less controlled. On the other hand, it is often assumed that employees are carefully screened and selected, and that they will wish to develop long-term careers with the company so will be careful not to do anything which may jeopardise this. It is also reassuring if someone is supervised by, and answerable to, some form of higher authority.

2. If you are answerable to someone else, it is only natural that the mental picture others form of your unseen superior is that of a person who must be, in every way, more impressive than yourself. This may help them to overlook any shortcomings you might have, in the same way that you might show a little more respect to an unimpressive junior executive if he represents Richard Branson. It is even more reassuring to outsiders

if you are perceived as being answerable not just to one person but to several – especially if they take the form of an official body such as a formal board of directors.

It is therefore a good idea to provide the company with a nominal chairman of the board, ideally with a different surname to yours (unless pursuing the strategy of pretending to be a family firm).

It is even more imposing if one can afford several non-executive directors. Having a proper board adds a great deal of dignity to a small company and gives it a more reliable image.

The sort of person who makes a good non-executive will probably have done the job before and will know what is expected (i.e., to keep quiet and let you get on with running the company in return for a small fee for turning up at the occasional meeting). Most non-executives are also good sources of information and business contacts, and can prove to be a very useful resource. There is no shortage of people willing to serve as non-executives (and most are much more affordable than you may think).

It can be lonely running your own business so having a regular forum where you can exchange ideas, ask for advice and share concerns may be helpful. Even bluffers need a shoulder to cry on sometimes. And if you have good news to share, it's nice to have someone with whom to share it.

FUNDING

The amount of capital you need to start or fund your business depends largely on the type of business you're in. If you're a service-based business, you probably won't need much capital to start with. You will need a phone, a desk in the proverbial spare bedroom and a smile while you dial. On the other hand, if your ambition is to revolutionise the ice cream industry by launching a brand-new type of ice cream that has to be made in Iceland with sacred cows' milk, you may need to raise some money to fund your dream (and pay for your prescription pills too). This is where you need OPM ('Other People's Money'). Three options are available to you:

1. Ask your bank for a loan. Unless you have some tangible asset like a property to offer as personal guarantee (the dreaded 'PG'), your odds of winning the lottery are better. Don't waste your time and energy filling in countless forms and trying to explain your business to your local branch manager, but do keep playing the lottery; after all, it does have an established track record in handing over money to people.

2. Ask friends and family for a loan or to invest in your business in return for some shares ('equity'). First, your friends and family need to have some money to spare. And second, they need to believe in you and your business. If you're looking for a loan, you need to offer a coupon (the interest you will be paying them during the life of the loan). More often than not, people taking a risk with a start-up business will want to own some shares in it. If things go well and the business is a runaway success, you will be a hero and your friends will be forever grateful for making them rich(er). If

on the other hand, your business fails, not only will you be experiencing personal financial pain, but your social life may become a little awkward too. You may become known as 'the guy who lost me 20 grand'. Then there are family reunions, never the most pleasant of occasions at the best of times. The fairly innocuous question 'How are you, Aunt Emma?' may be answered along the lines of 'I would be a lot better if you hadn't squandered my savings with that stupid venture of yours'. In an ideal world, you would be a member of the lucky sperm club and have a very wealthy family member who dotes on you and doesn't care about losing some of his or her vast cash pile.

3. Approach investors. There are two types:

   a) Private individuals, generally successful entre-preneurs who may have sold their own business and are looking for ventures to invest in and often to get involved with operationally too. They're called business angels. They can be really good news as they not only bring capital but their expertise, network of contacts and general business experience. Think of them as a successful, future you with grey hair (or no hair).

   b) Funds, either venture capital (if your business is young and normally technology-based) or private equity (if your business is more established and mature). The main downside is that they will probably have installed a bluffing detector outside their office and may be very hard to convince that you are worth investing in. In the case of venture capital, they will also want to get their hands on much more of the equity than you're willing to give away.

You can and should also look into obtaining a government business grant. These come in all shapes and sizes but they can be as difficult to get as a bank loan. Still, it is worth spending some time researching the usual suspects. Bluffers are not by definition cynical people but wouldn't it be nice to get something back from the government for a change?

If all your traditional fundraising efforts amount to no more than a myriad of useless meetings with people who have deep pockets but short arms, you could always try crowdfunding. Reassuringly, it does not involve walking up and down a high street, cap in hand and talking to strangers (God forbid!), it is merely an increasingly popular way of funding start-up or growing businesses by selling small amounts of equity to many investors. Most of the process is handled online so you won't even have to express your gratitude in person.

Funding is fundamental. Many businesses fail because the right funding is not in place when they need it. If you are raising money, ask for more, not less. It will also help people to take you more seriously (within limits – you don't want to end up in a straitjacket). Above all, be confident that you are asking for money for the right reasons and that you know exactly what you're going to do with it. Just like the government then…

When publishing giants
Random House and Penguin
merged, hopes were high that the
publishing world would be
graced with a Random Penguin.

A MATTER OF IDENTITY

WHAT'S IN A NAME?

Never underestimate the importance of a company's name. It is the first thing the customer comes into contact with.

You should not consider trading under the random set of letters and/or numbers that come with an off-the-shelf company (a company that someone already registered with Companies House and that is available to buy for a small fee). To do so is not merely a wasted opportunity but a symptom of laziness and lack of imagination. Company names based on letters or numbers might seem dynamic at first, but that soon wears off. They tend to be associated with the sort of entrepreneur whose companies don't last very long. They can also seem impersonal, unless based on a longer name which has been shortened over the years not by the company itself so much as by popular usage (BP, BT, M&S), which only tends to happen with large and illustrious organisations.

If you wish to stress reliability, rather than dynamism and originality, it is better to use a name that includes:

- a description of the type of business; and/or

- the geographical area in which you operate.

The implication is that you are established in that business or area, committed to it, and proud of it.

The drawback with such names is that they can prove restrictive if you ever diversify or expand. However, many large companies retain names based on products or areas that have long ceased to provide them with their main sources of income, because such names suggest tradition and continuity. For instance, it is fair to assume that Carphone Warehouse hasn't sold a car phone in a while. The bluffer who tries to simulate this would do well to think of a name that sounds as specialised, as localised and, ideally, as archaic as possible, so that no one could ever imagine it being confined to the trade and/or locality given in the name (like 'Old Sarum Saddlers Co Ltd').

Yet the most reliable companies tend to be those that include a personal or family name. There is no greater outward symbol of commitment to a company than a willingness to put one's own name on it.

There is a general assumption that no one would want to dishonour a company that bears one's own name – an assumption made by people who do not know that it is quite easy to transfer the name to another company in the event of an emergency. A problem only occurs if you sell the entire business to someone else and would have liked to use your own name again for the next one.

If you have adopted the wiser course of pretending that you are not the company but merely a small, if significant, cog in a larger corporate machine, you could name the company after someone else entirely or let your imagination run wild and come up with a name of your choice or even making. First things first, get together a few friends for an evening of uninhibited brainstorming over a few bottles of wine and give the exercise your all. Not only is it great fun, it may also save the thousands of pounds that an agency would charge you to come up with a name for your company. When Price Waterhouse and Coopers & Lybrand, two of the global tax and accountancy firms, merged years ago, they allegedly paid brand naming consultants a fortune to come up with a name for the merged entity…before settling on PricewaterhouseCoopers. Who said accountants lacked imagination? And when publishing giants Random House and Penguin merged recently, hopes were high that the publishing world would be graced with a Random Penguin. Alas, in another display of inventiveness, the more demure Penguin Random House won the day.

Whatever the outcome of your booze-fuelled naming session, it is always a good idea to check a few things: is the name you've settled on already taken? Is the right domain name available? Thankfully, the dot-com suffix no longer rules the web as many other suffixes are now available, but it is worth spending time online to check that you're not infringing other people's intellectual property. Running a basic trademark search will save you thousands of pounds in possible litigation further down the line. It would be a shame to have spent all that money and effort on building a brand and successful business only to discover that you weren't allowed to use that brand name in the first place. It is becoming increasingly hard to find a name that isn't already being used, doesn't mean something offensive in Japanese or Russian (especially if Japan or Russia are big target markets for you) and where the domain name is available (and not for a king's ransom from one of those cyber or domain squatters). This is the reason why many start-up companies choose to make a name up and get on with it. It is very tempting to agonise over a name for weeks, but it is wise to resist that temptation and just get on with the business of business. Familiarity will breed acceptance (admittedly, it can also breed contempt, but let's remain positive here) and after a while, people will stop trying to figure out what it means (assuming they cared in the first place). For instance, who can say they gave much thought to the name Hertz last time they were queuing for a rental car at a busy airport? Painful, isn't it?

CREATING AN IMAGE

Now you have a name, you need a logo – in other words, a brand identity. It's essentially the same thing but designers can charge a lot more money by helping you with your brand identity rather than just drawing a pretty logo. Again, a logo matters insofar as you will have to live with it for a long time and people love commenting on them, especially if the business is starting up. A brand designer will ask you questions like: 'If you were a car/colour/animal, etc., what would you be? (yes, really). If your answer is 'I'm a black polo pony driving an Aston Martin', there is a good chance you'll end up with a very upmarket and luxurious-looking logo. If you answer 'I'm a pink elephant driving a Mini', don't complain if you end up with a pink logo. Whatever your designer comes up with, you are unlikely to be happy the first time you see it and you will want to see many further interpretations, show them to a number of different people for feedback, and try to reach a consensus. Some people may also recommend that you organise some focus groups on anything from the name of your business to its logo or market positioning. This is a recommendation worth following… if you enjoy wasting time and money. This is your business, you're the driving force behind it, you should know what your customers want and you shouldn't need to spend thousands of pounds to have outsiders telling you how it is. You're a bluffer, remember?

As with the name of your business, don't obsess and prevaricate. Sooner rather than later it will be time to draw a line in the sand, choose one logo and say: 'that's it, from this day forward, for better, for worse, for richer, for poorer, in sickness and in health, until ruin do us part.' You and your logo are going to have to live together for as long as the business is alive (unless you really enjoy throwing money down the drain, in which case you could undertake a rebranding exercise at some point down the line). With very few exceptions, logos do not make or break businesses. Companies with terrible logos have flourished whilst others with impeccable branding credentials have foundered and disappeared into oblivion. Find a logo you like and get on with the business of making money and having fun.

Having said that, first impressions do count. If your business starts off by making a bad impression – or, even worse, by making no impression at all – it will take years to correct, if it can be corrected. Most businesses do not have years to spare.

Some people might be tempted to hedge their bets – to hold resources back from the launch of a business in case it becomes necessary to pay for a relaunch. Such people do not belong in business.

The true entrepreneur must be prepared to bet everything on his or her judgement. It is difficult enough for a start-up business to make a big enough splash to be noticed, even with all its available resources. If those resources are divided in order to pay for a series of tiny ripples, instead of one big splash, it is even more unlikely that the business will make any sort of impression. Moreover, any relaunch will inevitably be more difficult to carry off than the original launch because it will have to cost at least as much as the one that failed and, in fear of further failure, probably more.

Most start-ups are not noted for having large piles of spare cash lying around, so what money there is has to be spent effectively. The bright bluffer will spend it where it can be seen.

FIRST IMPRESSIONS

In most businesses, the first thing a customer will see of your company will not be you, your staff or your premises, but either your website or your letterhead.

It would be easy to dismiss the importance of the letterhead in this increasingly digital world, and even to laugh at its mere mention. However, many businesses still send large quantities of letters – and the way they look will speak volumes about the business, like it or not.

The successful business will use good-quality paper, but not too good. The ultra-stiff paper, usually coloured and embossed, has lately become the preserve of the more dubious end of the financial services market. You might as well add the words 'Do Not Do Business With These People' in red on the top.

And as for business cards, your name on the little rectangle should be as discreet as possible. Business cards – indeed, all sales and marketing material – should follow the same corporate identity. This simply means making sure that all material put out by your business has the same logo, layout and lettering. It makes it easier for everyone (including yourself) to remember which company you are. Business cards are very inexpensive these days (outfits like Moo.com do a very good job despite having a name not traditionally associated with stationery). So just follow the herd for once and spend your hard-earned cash elsewhere.

At the risk of stating the obvious, never a bad technique for a novice bluffer, you also need a website. A lot of what was said earlier about names and logos also holds true for your website. You could spend weeks debating the right font, colour scheme, layout, etc. instead of getting on with business. A website just needs to be informative, accurate and state clearly the business you're in. Cluttered websites should be avoided at all costs. If you must emulate something, you could do worse than Google's home page. It hasn't served them too badly. These days, websites can be built cheaply and quickly so avoid the trap of remortgaging your house for an all-singing, all-dancing site which you will almost certainly want to change in a few months' time.

♛

A good PA will be your partner in bluff: it is not easy to believe something when only one person says it, but it becomes more credible when two people appear to believe it.

The overpriced web designer/developer will, of course, offer to create the perfect website, with lots of bells and whistles. He – they are almost invariably male – will want to install all the latest gimmicks that will make your site 'stand out' and attract attention.

This is exactly what your business does not need. The point is that your site does not need to 'stand out' to attract attention – after all, if people see it, it means they are already there and their attention has already been attracted. It is far more important to make sure that it can be accessed by everyone, including people other than web designers and developers. Keep it simple. No one likes having to download new software to navigate a flashy site.

Your site must also be easy to read. A busy home page with lots of words and pictures is distracting. Too many bright, contrasting colours may even make it look like a porn site (or what we are led to understand they look like). Better to stick to a single background colour, a couple of key pictures that sum up your business and a list of the contents of the website.

When building your website, bear in mind SEO (Search Engine Optimisation). These three letters can make a lot of difference to your business by pushing it up search engine rankings and thereby giving you and your company a much better chance of being discovered. The Internet is a crowded place these days.

The bluffer's goal is to make his or her website one that will be bookmarked and visited frequently. This means providing a lot of general information, keeping it up to date, and putting in a lot of links to other relevant sites. Be open to banners – advertising links to other sites – but not at the expense of the overall style and credibility of your own. It is a good idea to have your banners on other people's sites. This may cost you, and you will need to be selective with this form of advertising, but some sites may be open to reciprocal arrangements: they put their banners on your site and you put yours on theirs; everybody wins. Look particularly for non-commercial sites that might be interested in your line of business. So, for example, a car owners' club site might be open to having your car-parts business banner on their site in return for putting theirs on yours.

Keep surfing the web yourself to check out relevant sites, as things change quickly. And above all, keep checking your own website. This may sound odd but it is amazing how many big businesses spend a fortune on fancy web developers to build a state-of-the-art site and then never look at it again. As a result, information is soon out of date or irrelevant and can make the business lose credibility. If you make sure there is always something new on your site, potential customers will have a reason to return.

A PRESTIGIOUS ADDRESS (WITHOUT THE EXPENSE OF HAVING TO BE THERE)

It is not necessary to rent an outrageously priced office in a fashionable area when all one wants is the address. It is fairly easy to obtain a convenience address; the advanced bluffer might want to have more than one (e.g., New York, Tokyo, Paris – any place where it might be deemed advantageous for your particular business). Anyone wanting to meet you personally will be just as happy meeting at their own place or on neutral ground, such as a hotel lobby or a restaurant.

You might also consider using the services of a 'virtual office', which will provide you with a human answering service, a prestigious address (Mayfair, St James's…) and various other services which reduce traditional office overheads while conveying the definite impression of business credibility. You could also employ your mum to do much the same thing (tax-deductible, of course) but the address might not be quite in the same league.

AN EXPERIENCED PA

If you choose to go down the traditional office route, a good personal assistant is more than a labour-saving device and status symbol. The fact that you are an employer – even if you only have one employee – rather than a lone wolf will gain you standing straight away.

A good PA will be your partner in bluff: it is not easy to believe something when only one person says it, but it becomes more credible when two people appear to believe it.

When marketing, you are a sportsman
engaged on the greatest hunt of all…
First of all, you must identify your
quarry; then you come into contact
with it; and only you can bring it home.

MARKETING
AND OPERATIONS

THE MARKETING MIX

'Marketing' is simply the word bluffers have coined to describe the grubby business of 'selling'. The bluffer will never admit this. Indeed, the word 'selling' should never pass your lips, and even 'marketing' should not be used in mixed company (i.e., in front of prospective customers or clients). So if:

Marketing = Selling, and

Selling = Business, and

Business = Bluff,

logic dictates that

Marketing = Bluff.

However, you should never be caught bluffing when selling because:

a) If a sale is found to be based on selective information, it could be void by law. The buyer could claim his or her money back and the seller could be liable to civil, or even criminal, action.

b) It's unsporting.

When marketing, you are a sportsman engaged on the greatest hunt of all. As with any hunt there are rules, and there is a proper order in which things are done. First of all, you must identify your quarry; then you come into contact with it; and only you can bring it home. Thus:

1. **Market research** identifies the customer.

2. **Sales and Marketing** makes contact with the customer.

3. **Distribution** delivers the product or service.

MARKET RESEARCH

In the old days, 'market research' consisted of someone with a clipboard asking people in the street, who were busy trying to avoid them, what they thought of a particular product or service. People with clipboards still exist on our streets but they are now less likely to be carrying out market research and more likely to be intent on persuading you to set up a direct debit in favour of a particular charity. They are called, perhaps uncharitably, charity muggers, or 'chuggers'.

These days, 'consumer surveying' is done mainly by phone or, increasingly and more cost-effectively, online. However, the bluffer will view market research as a far broader process, involving the formulation of strategy, new product development, test marketing and the gathering of a great deal of information of which canvassing consumers is only one part.

There are two reasons why you should adopt this broad approach:

1. Consumer surveying is still too expensive for small or start-up businesses and may be irrelevant if the business does not deal with a mass market.

2. It allows you to work out exactly who your customer is, and how he or she is best approached. A business dealing with a small number of relatively high-spending customers ought to have a completely different marketing strategy from one with a large number of relatively low spenders.

Only when you are sure where your customers can be found should you start trying to attract their attention.

SALES AND MARKETING

Sales and marketing includes anything that might attract the customer's weary eyes towards your product. This covers a wide variety of sins from point of sale (POS) displays to alleged 'competitions', 'special offers' and 'sales' that go on forever.

Advertising

The small business can forget about mass-media campaigns; to penetrate the collective consciousness and establish your product as a 'brand' name is far too expensive (and cannot be guaranteed). Advertising is pointless unless you are prepared to do it properly, which means spending more money than most start-up businesses are ever likely to have.

Having said that, some businesses have managed to establish a brand without spending the huge amounts of money they didn't have by being smart and doing things differently. Social media is a very tricky beast to tame but it does open up immense possibilities to the creative bluffer. Some blogs started in the proverbial spare bedroom have flourished to become bona fide businesses.

Press and public relations

This should appeal to the subtle bluffer who enjoys the idea of marketing by pretending not to market.

By going down the editorial route rather than the advertising route, you can promote your business without the cost of actually paying for advertising.

Journalists should become your friends. Contrary to legend, few of them can be bribed with drink (although few can resist a good lunch), but good social relations help to keep channels of communication open. So do regular briefings (especially if spiced with some good gossip – feel free to refer to it as 'market intelligence' – whether on or off the record) in addition to putting absolutely anything that might give your business publicity into a press release.

The press release should not err on the side of modesty:

(Headline) EXECUTIVE TEAM STRENGTHENED
(Sub head) New transparent wall maintenance operative joins Universal Widgets
(Text) One of Barchester's most progressive and ambitious

companies has announced the appointment of AN Other who joins an experienced and dynamic team…
(Translation: Universal Widgets has just taken on a new window cleaner.)

Other examples of useful headlines on press releases:

JOBS AT RISK
(The standard line when a public authority threatens to do something the company doesn't like.)

LOCAL FIRM IN TALKS WITH US GIANT
(They phoned to ask about the price.)

LOCAL FIRM SIGNS CONTRACT WITH US GIANT
(We actually sold them something.)

US GIANT & LOCAL FIRM LINK UP
(They gave us a local sales agency.)

US GIANT & LOCAL FIRM IN PARTNERSHIP DEAL
(The sales agency is a joint venture: we split the profits.)

LOCAL FIRM TO TAKE OVER US GIANT?
(Well, anyone can speculate, can't they?)

Direct mailing

The bluffer's best hope. A letter need reveal little about the sender: the recipient does not know if it is from a big or a small business.

It is possible to buy a good mailing list suited to your business needs – a good investment if you can afford it – but it might be too expensive. If so, you can create your own using trade directories, local business directories, electoral rolls, online research and networks like LinkedIn, the leading social network for professionals.

If you do not have the name and exact title of the addressee (always preferable), use the most prestigious title you can imagine each functionary having – e.g., if you are selling office supplies, 'the director of administration'. When in doubt, go straight to the top and write to 'the chief executive', the form of address most likely to get your letter to the real power, whatever his or her true title.

Direct sales

In many businesses, especially those whose customers are other businesses (known as 'business-to-business', or B2B), a great deal is done through personal contact. Turning a non-business contact into a business one is a skill that can be learnt only by experience. It helps if an entrepreneur gets around as much as possible and becomes involved in organisations to which prospective customers belong. Join as many as your resources permit.

Do not imagine that fellow members will suddenly provide you with business just because you are one of them, but if you make them aware of your business, the day may come when you could be given the chance to put in a competitive quote simply because they happen to know you personally.

E-commerce

The Internet was designed for bluffers running their own business. It has given them the level playing field they have always craved. Online, the biggest and smallest businesses in the world are both boiled down to a small screen. Whether you spend millions on marketing or are somehow getting it for free, it makes no difference. Your ability to impress depends solely on your ability to convince those looking at that screen that you have something they might need.

It is easy to pretend online that yours is a big business – no one has to see your office or your employees – but, paradoxically, the one time it is easy to do may be the one time that it is not necessary.

It seems that the only place the small business does not need to look like a big business is online. People who buy on sites like eBay rather like the idea that they are dealing with a 'Mom-and-Pop' operation; there are cases of large established companies pretending not to be in order to appeal to a broader audience.

Social media

Social media marketing is a hard topic to avoid these days, and has been the subject of much hype. Some businesses have had great success with it, but others have gone in with high expectations that were, almost inevitably, disappointed. Whether it is right for you depends on the nature of your business, the norms of the sector and how it fits with the image you want to project. If you are in a trendy business like media or technology – and it seems that half of start-ups these days are themselves social media-related – it is practically compulsory, but an agricultural feed outfit, for example, would be unwise to rely on it too much.

Social media is not relevant to all businesses so you must first decide whether it is relevant to your business. If you decide to use social media, you must then commit to doing it properly or not bother at all. You need to keep your content up to date; if you get out of the habit of posting or tweeting regularly, people may assume that you are no longer in business or that your business isn't doing very well. Your content has to be lively and interesting, too; it is not enough simply to 'tweet' new products as they become available. If you do not feel you can maintain a good standard, best to avoid active social media marketing altogether.

DISTRIBUTION

Think of distribution not as part of the selling process but as a continuation of the process of promotion. The packaging, the company name on the delivery van, the physical presence of the product itself – all are forms of advertising.

Delivery should always be accompanied by fanfare, even in businesses without a product in the traditional sense. A construction firm will put a large sign outside a building it is repairing; an accountant will usually deliver accounts in a binder with the firm's name on it; and an estate agent will send you a basket of homemade cookies the day you move into your new home (in your dreams).

OPERATIONS

Having gone to all that trouble to sell a product or service, it seems rather unfair that you have to provide it as well. Unfortunately, most customers tend to insist on getting something in return for their money, unreasonable cads that they are.

So the question is: 'What product?' To which the true entrepreneur will reply: 'Anything I can sell.' Nevertheless, you ought to have a main or principal product of some sort. It provides you with a ready answer to the question: 'What business are you in?'

An evasive reply will make everyone assume you must be into something shady. As an entrepreneur, you will have enough trouble trying to establish the reputation of your business without people thinking that you must be a gunrunner.

When selecting your principal product, consider the extent to which it can be used as the base for a broader range of products.

Having selected a product, your next question is how to produce it. The answer is: you don't. As a rule, your new business should never actually produce a product. Production costs money: selling makes money. Production is a pain; it takes up time (better spent selling) and money (spent on plant, machinery and labour). Even if you reduce your costs through vigorous self-denial and constant vigilance, you are unlikely to be able to match the low unit costs, or quality, of mass production and economies of scale.* The answer is to sell something produced by someone else. You can do one of the following:

a) Obtain agency agreements to sell the products of another company.

* 'Economies of scale' is business-school speak for 'Big is Beautiful'.

b) Employ manufacturers to do your production for you on a sub-contract basis.

There are thousands of variations on the above, most notably the mutual reference arrangement which means that both you and your producer act as agents for each other. In general, you cannot have too many business contacts, however casual, whether they are prepared to pay you commission to sell their products, prepared to sell your products in return for commission, or willing to produce for you at need.

♛

The ideal business has no capital, no stock, no premises and, above all, no employees.

It is worth remembering that the word 'entrepreneur', loosely translated, is French for 'middleman'.

The ideal business has no capital, no stock, no premises and, above all, no employees. True, there is a limit to the amount of money you will make without them, but you may well decide that, beyond a certain point, the extra cash really is not worth the extra hassle. This is particularly true these days when almost everything is subject to government regulation and you can be sued for almost everything else.

The bigger business can hire someone to push the paper around. In the smaller business, it all falls on the boss –

who has better things to do. The focus of the entrepreneur must always be on exchanging products or services for money, and anything that distracts from that, like actually running a business, should be avoided where possible.

Experience of your own business will end the delusion of most taxpayers. It is one long succession of encounters with the taxman under different pretexts.

THE THREE BURDENS
OF BUSINESS

All businesses, big or small, established or start-up (but the small start-up disproportionately) must bear three burdens.

The first, and easily the most visible, is the burden of giving money directly to the government in the form of taxes, contributions, levies, fees or whatever other euphemisms they might use. Although it is the best known of the three burdens, it may also be the lightest.

The second burden is the 'costs of compliance' with laws and regulations. Although this involves no direct payments to the government, it is very much a result of demands by the government and can be just as expensive.

Yet the third burden of business may be the heaviest. It is the wholly unnecessary hassle, stress, irritation, distraction and frustration involved when one has to deal with unpleasant bureaucrats, read incomprehensible regulations, fill in badly designed forms, and ask the same basic question again and again to get the simplest information, when one could be thinking of and implementing new business ideas, marketing strategies and operations plans to improve profitability, provide goods and services other people want, increase national prosperity, generate employment for those who need it and generally make the world a better place for everyone.

TAX

Jean-Baptiste Colbert, Minister of Finance to French king Louis XIV, likened tax policy to plucking a goose: the ideal is to maximise the amount of feathers while minimising the amount of hissing.

Governments have become very good at this. Very few citizens realise how much tax they actually pay, directly or indirectly, because governments extract it surreptitiously via business. Yet it all comes out of the same pot in the end, and the taxpayer may be paying indirectly through more expensive goods and services what he is not paying directly through open deductions from his pay packet.

Experience of your own business will end the delusion of most taxpayers. It is one long succession of encounters with the taxman under different pretexts.

First of all, before the business has made a penny in sales or profits, there are a host of 'above-the-line' taxes that add to the cost of doing business. There may be taxes on the development of land, possibly through planning or zoning fees, and on the purchase of land, called 'stamp duty' in the UK. Once the business has acquired land, it may also have to pay an annual property tax on it, known as 'business rates' in the UK. There are also charges for a huge range of registrations and permits, which function as taxes by another name. Your initial purchases of stock and capital equipment may or may not be exempt from sales tax, called VAT in the UK; the system of exemptions is notoriously incomprehensible, as is the system of capital allowances for corporation tax purposes. You may also have to hand over a payroll tax, known as 'employer's contributions to national insurance' in the UK, on employees' salaries, in addition to what the employees pay themselves. Yes, there really is a tax on generating employment.

If a business manages to scrape together the money to get through all those preliminaries and actually begin selling things – but still before it makes a profit – it must hand over any sales taxes or VAT on what it sells. The theory is that the business does not pay this but only collects it from the customer on behalf of the government. What the theory ignores is the fact that it all comes from the same pot. In this case, the pot is the customer and the customer has finite resources, so to accommodate a sales tax, the business has to choose between passing it on entirely, which increases prices and therefore decreases sales, or absorbing all or part of it directly, which increases costs and therefore decreases profit margins. In practice, most businesses in a competitive environment are forced to find a balance which usually involves a bit of both. Either way, there is a cost to the business.

If, despite all this, the business finally makes a profit, that profit is taxed. A sole proprietor pays income tax. A company pays corporation tax.

When whatever is left of a company's profits are

transferred to the owner, income tax must be paid on what takes the form of salary and dividends (the latter being the most tax-efficient way to receive an income from business activities). Capital gains tax (CGT) is payable if or when shares in the business are sold at a profit. A complex system of allowances may mitigate 'double taxation', but there is always leakage in the taxman's favour.

Then, when at last you have the well-deserved rewards of your efforts in your own pocket, you pay sales tax or VAT whenever you spend it, like anyone else. If you invest it instead, you pay tax on the return on investment. When you die, your children pay death duties or inheritance tax on your estate.

A Welsh industrialist once calculated that his business had to make £10,000 in sales for him to take home enough to pay for his wife's haircut. Perhaps she was fussy about her hair.

The annoying thing is not just handing over to lazy bureaucrats a large slice of what you have earned through your own diligence, self-sacrifice and initiative with no help from them – indeed, often in the face of their active obstruction. No, the really annoying thing is that they expect you to manage the process for them. If you make any errors, they penalise you, but you cannot penalise them if they make a mistake – as they often do.

You have little practical alternative but to hire an accountant to deal with it all. Accountancy itself has become something of a bluff because the tax system is now so complex that not even an accountant can master it all, but it does at least give you someone to blame if a mistake is made. Of course, the fact that it is not your fault will not make a bit of difference to the taxman, who will still come after you without mercy or restraint.

THE COSTS OF COMPLIANCE

This can cover a wide variety of punishing legal and financial obligations, from the need to hire an accountant to deal with an unnecessarily complex tax system to the need to draft employee handbooks and keep detailed employee records in case you are ever sued by someone you've asked to leave your business. The greatest of these costs of compliance is not the waste of money but the waste of a far more precious and finite business asset: your own time.

These are the ones to look out for:

PAYROLL

Payroll is a pain at the best of times. You can trust government to make it worse. As well as paying and administering their own taxes, businesses usually have to administer the income tax payments of any employees.In many countries this includes a form of additional income tax that is called something else, like 'social insurance', 'national insurance' or 'social security'.

Most of these schemes are pure bluff. The theory is that the payments go into a separate fund that will later provide pensions for the employees' retirement, or benefits during periods of unemployment or sickness. Yet these funds are an accounting fiction. The money paid into them is not invested for the future but paid out immediately to meet current obligations.

If a private sector pension or insurance fund did that, it would be called a Ponzi scheme and the managers would be put in prison. Since these schemes are underwritten

---

♛

The greatest of the costs of compliance is not the waste of money but the waste of a far more precious and finite business asset: your own time.

---

by the government's general funds, both the employers' and employees' contributions are essentially income taxes pretending not to be income taxes. Colbert would have loved them.

PENSIONS
Many larger companies have long run pension schemes for their employees. Some are major players in the pensions sector in their own right and have built up considerable expertise. Most businesses, however, are in the business they are in and no other. Their knowledge is confined to the sector in which they earn their living. Unless this happens to be the financial services sector, they should not be expected to have any real knowledge of pensions.

This has not stopped the trend for Western governments

to make it compulsory for businesses to make arrangements for their employees' pensions. And since the real-time information rule was introduced in the UK, employers (or their accountant, bookkeeper or payroll bureau) now have to:

- send details to HMRC every time they pay an employee, at the time they pay them; and

- use payroll software to send this information electronically as part of their routine payroll process.

All this is another example of the great bluff pulled off by politicians in convincing the voters that they care about something – in this case, pensions – when all they are really doing is dumping the problem on business.

The same is true of...

HEALTHCARE INSURANCE

Once a perk offered by major employers, the provision of healthcare insurance is now increasingly compulsory in many countries, even for businesses – the vast majority – with no knowledge or experience of the sector.

Most small businesses end up using the biggest provider by default. The biggest is rarely the best or even the most cost-efficient, but using them provides a strong defence if employees complain about the quality: 'I'm terribly sorry if you're not happy with the quality of the healthcare on offer, but we did go with the market leader.'

INSURANCE

Many businesses are wary of insurance. Business is a risk

and you must accept that. There is no insuring against many of the things that can happen, and where there is, it may not be worth the large premiums – especially when one has experience of how insurance companies try to wheedle their way out of their obligations when a payout is due.

Sometimes there is no option, especially where a third party is likely to be involved. Third-party insurance is compulsory in most jurisdictions if you are operating a vehicle on the highway. There is strict liability under English and Scots law for injuries on your property, so a proper public liability policy is essential. Product liability insurance is practically compulsory in the European Union. Employer's liability insurance is mandatory in the UK, except on a nominal employee who happens to own the company. The US equivalent is 'workers' comp'. Some specialist sectors or professions require professional indemnity insurance if you are to be allowed to practise.

Your best bet is usually a combined policy. Take advice from independent brokers, but always remember that they have a vested interest in overinsuring you. Always check the small print; do not just read it – it is probably indecipherable anyway – but ask questions and get answers in plain English, ideally in writing.

ENVIRONMENTAL REGULATION

As a rule, it is not a good idea to initiate contact with bureaucrats until you have no choice. The local environmental authorities might be an exception. You need to know in advance what counts as standard commercial waste and what is potentially hazardous; you might be surprised by how wide the definitions can be. This applies even to businesses that do not think of themselves as 'industrial'.

Needless to say, the bluffer must present an image to these people as being green in every sense of the word. Contrary to some anti-business propaganda, the vast majority of businesses these days tend to accept the need for environmental regulation. They ask only that it be enforced equally so that they can compete on a level playing field.

The same applies to…

HEALTH AND SAFETY

No one wants to return to the days of children being sent up chimneys and miners relying on canaries to warn about gas, but there is a growing feeling that some of the things being done in the once-honourable name of health and safety are absurd.

There are two different traditions of 'elf'n'safety' at work. The European tradition emphasises regulation in advance. The US tradition relies more on litigation after the event. The two approaches reflect different cultures: Europeans are used to governments legislating in detail to control their lives; Americans demand more freedom of choice but enforce responsibility for that choice through massive claims for damages.

The two approaches are coming together, so you can now

expect both excessive regulation and excessive litigation. It is worth noting that some of the most notorious examples of overcaution that are giving health and safety an unnecessarily bad name tend to be the result of paranoid fear of litigation rather than direct regulation.

TRAINING

Businesses need qualified and trained employees. The problem is that no one wants to pay for their training or carry them while they are learning on the job – especially since they tend to leave for better-paid jobs as soon as they become really useful.

Some jurisdictions try to counter this by making it compulsory for all businesses to contribute to training, or training levies – yet another word for taxes – but small business, having less to offer the newly qualified, usually loses as a result of these measures.

LITIGATION

It seems that employees will sue their employers or former employers over anything these days. To be fair, if you want to act like Captain Bligh, you have only yourself to blame if some latter-day Fletcher Christian launches the highly lucrative modern equivalent of a mutiny, but most smaller business types tend to be friendly, easy-going people, possibly only in business in the first place because they enjoy interacting with others. They can be as much victims of a bullying employee as the other way round. If you think you may have a trouble-maker on your hands, start keeping a written record of all incidents, however trivial. It might sound excessive but you might need it.

In general, litigation is rarely worth the stress, the distraction and the waste of time and money involved, even if you win. Avoid it if you can. Settle if you must. You may feel strongly on a point of principle, but you will find that the legal system has changed little since Dickens's time and cares little about points of principle. Unhappily, any barrack-room lawyer with whom you fall out will be only too aware of that.

♛

> Businesses need qualified and trained employees. The problem is that no one wants to pay for their training.

ADMINISTRATION

Business is supposed to be serious, so the bluffer in business must appear serious about it. This may take quite a bit of bluff because there is no denying that, for people who enjoy a challenge, there is a lot of fun to be had in business – until recently, that is.

For neither can it be denied that there is one aspect of business that sucks the joy out of it. Administration – bluffer-speak for paperwork – is tedious to discuss but even more tedious to do. The mere mention of the subject is so depressing that the first edition of this guide in 1992 omitted it altogether in the hope that, if we ignored it, it would go away.

Unsurprisingly, this has not happened. On the contrary, the last 20 years have seen an exponential growth in bureaucracy and red tape in most countries. This can be seen physically, in the increase in the size of tax codes and volumes of new laws. A fairly well-educated person, reading during standard working hours at normal speed and stopping to cross-reference points in order to understand them fully, could not read the UK or US tax codes in the year before a new one comes out. It's not unlike painting the Forth Bridge. Yet the law works on the assumption that we have memorised them all, and it will penalise any error without mercy. In the same way, it is almost certain that no one human being has ever read all the laws and by-laws passed in most 'developed' jurisdictions in a year, but they all apply to us nonetheless.

So there is no avoiding it, and therefore no avoiding discussing it. Nor is there much scope for bluffing our way out of it. If anything, the whole business world is the victim of a giant bluff, as the politicians and bureaucrats have hidden the extent to which they get us to do their work for them and make us pay for the privilege.

PEOPLE YOU CANNOT AVOID

THE BANK MANAGER

The bank manager is arguably the most powerful person in the world of the smaller business.

The bluffer will immediately grasp that the key is to convince the bank manager that you have tons of money, and don't really need to borrow more, but would like to do so anyway. There are, of course, two slight problems with this:

1. Any sensible person (and bank managers are always the most sensible of people) will wonder why you want to borrow money if you say you already have enough.

2. Your bank manager probably has a better idea of how much money you have than you do.

So trying to bluff a bank manager is a bit like trying to out-eat a sumo wrestler: it is theoretically possible but just not very likely. But there are steps you can take that will put you at less of a disadvantage:

1. Think big

The same bank that sends you emails or letters if you are a few pence over your overdraft limit seems to be more than happy to lend millions to some of the most dubious businessmen in the world. This is because banks assume that someone who asks for £100,000 is used to dealing with such sums and is not worried about paying it back, while someone who asks for £100 is obviously a small-time loser. So it pays to overestimate your needs.

The bank manager will wish to demonstrate his control by giving you less than you ask for. So if you want £10,000, ask for £30,000. (He or she will halve the sum, but you will inevitably find that you need half as much again as you thought you did.)

2. Exploit your business plan

The figures in your plan should support your position that you are doing very nicely and expect to be doing even better as a result of the business, but can foresee times when you might, under certain circumstances, have temporary cash-flow difficulties. You want a secure credit facility just in case. Bank managers adore cautious people.

3. Increase your credit rating over time

Borrow money when you don't need it in order to demonstrate your ability to pay it back. Having proved your ability with small loans, gradually increase their size. Your record will not save you if things go bad, but a large loan facility may help to keep your options open.

THE ACCOUNTANT

A good accountant can be defined as one who saves you almost as much in taxes as he charges in fees.

Most entrepreneurs treat their accountants as their Father Confessor – friend, guide and Fount of All Wisdom. This can be true, but don't follow any advice blindly. When choosing an accountant, beware of the type who when asked the sum of two plus two answers 'how much do you want it to be?'

THE CONSULTANT

Businesses are increasingly using consultants in every functional area. Their role is to deliver specialist skills from a different perspective, supposedly. If you need help in any aspect of your business, then it's a certain bet that there is a management consultant hanging around in reception who can help. As a bluffer you might find a consultant rather convenient – someone who can actually do the bluffing for you. It not only works quite effectively, but also helps you to learn from a master of the art... which is of course the problem.

Consultancy is an occupation that attracts more than its share of BS artists. Even the good ones may overcharge and may waste a lot of time 'learning about your business' (which you are paying for). You could end up with results that are of no use at all, and a long, wordy, vague report that requires a PhD in cryptology to decipher. God forbid that you should find yourself involved in any sort of litigation, but the barrister's 'counsel's opinion' is an example of the most advanced sort of all of these cryptic exercises. Rest assured that it will identify the problem by plumbing hitherto unexplored depths of prolixity, but will it offer you a solution? You've got more chance of knitting fog.

> As a bluffer you might find
> a consultant rather convenient –
> someone who can actually do
> the bluffing for you.

Hiring the right sort of consultant, however, could still be the answer to a lot of problems and is usually a better option than hiring new staff on permanent contracts, with all the legal and administrative hassle that it entails. You just have to keep your consultant on a tight rein. Define exactly what you want and then get the consultant to repeat it back to you very slowly so you can be sure that you are understood. Do not allow consultants to go wandering off, giving you what they think you need rather than what you want. This is what they like to do. Your job is to keep them on track.

THE PERSONAL ASSISTANT

You might, if you're very good, bluff your banker, your accountant, even your family, but you will never bluff your personal assistant. Nor should you try. He or she must be your ally in carrying off your bluff.

All contact must be made through your PA. You must be unavailable much of the time, even if you're not actually doing anything. This will mean much more work for you since, for example, you will have to return the calls (via your PA) because you were 'not there' at the time. But the impression will be that you are devoting yourself almost exclusively to the serious business of making money.

Routine administration takes up a great deal of time since it has to be done whether the business is making a lot of money or not. By relieving you of these tasks, the PA lets you get on with what you are supposed to be doing, even if this means that you end up helping your PA to do the work, rather than the other way round.

THE REST OF THE WORLD

Everyone else falls into one of two categories:

1. people who give you money – customers and clients; or

2. people you give money to – suppliers, employees, advisers.

Both should be dealt with in exactly the same way. They must be approached with a display of self-confidence so absolute that they are forced to assume you must have something to be confident about.

If you can convince enough people, you may one day really have something to be confident about. On that day, when your small business is the big business it always pretended to be, you can admit how small you once were, and how you built your giant multinational from a shed in your back garden.

Just make sure you don't tell anyone about the garden shed until it is safely buried in the concrete of your glass tower head office.

PEOPLE YOU CAN EMULATE

By now, you should be able to hold your own in the company of distinguished business owners, but if you actually want to start your own business and need a little inspiration to get you on your way, here is a list of 10 successful start-ups and the story of how they began.

INNOCENT DRINKS

Innocent was founded in 1999 by three Cambridge University graduates, Richard Reed, Adam Balon and Jon Wright. The three friends were on a snowboarding holiday when they decided to stop talking about starting a business and actually start doing something about it.

After coming up with some smoothie recipes and spending £500 on fruit and blenders, the trio set up a drinks stall at a music festival in London. Customers were asked to put their empty cup in a 'yes' or 'no' bin depending on whether they thought the three should quit their jobs to make smoothies. At the end of the festival the 'YES' bin was full, with only three cups in the 'NO' bin, so they resigned from their positions in advertising and management consultancy the next day. They wrote a business plan, then they wrote it again 11 times. As they admitted themselves, it was rather boring. Every bank, venture capitalist and private investor they approached turned them down. Eventually an American 'business angel' (*see* 'Funding' page 41) put up £250,000. In total, it took 15 months from the initial idea to bringing the product to market. At first the brand was known as Fast Tractor, then Hungry Aphid, then Nude, then Naked. Sensibly, they settled on Innocent.

The three founders have now sold more than 90% of the business to Coca-Cola, a company long associated with unadulterated, healthy, additive-free beverages…

Lesson: Not all fruit is low-hanging. Be prepared to reach higher.

CAMBRIDGE SATCHELS

The Cambridge Satchel Company was founded by Julie Deane at her kitchen table in 2008. Her motivation was certainly original. She had promised her daughter she would make enough money to send her to a school where she would be happier.

After brainstorming a few ideas with her mother (but restricted by a meagre budget of £600), Deane decided that she would start a satchel company, with products initially aimed at schoolchildren. After spending a lot of time on the internet, she managed to source a leather manufacturer and an initial prototype was fashioned.

By persevering with a strategy of online guerilla marketing (business bluffers will know that that is anything involving imaginative lateral thinking and minimum cost), and slowly but surely building relationships with magazine and newspaper shopping editors, opportunity came knocking in September 2011. The UK magazine *Elle* requested that she make a fluorescent satchel to be included in one of their fashion features. Deane obliged, and also sent the model out to a host of fashion bloggers. This didn't go unnoticed. The buzz surrounding the fluorescent 'it' satchels led to Saks and Bloomingdales putting in orders, and also resulted in a business deal with Google.

The company quickly went from making three hand-stitched bags per week to 1500, and now has an impressive turnover and is growing fast.

Lesson: If your idea leads to a better idea, wrap it, tag it and bag it.

MAGMATIC

Magmatic is a children's travel product company founded by designer Rob Law, most famous for a wheeled suitcase known as the Trunki. The idea for the part-suitcase/part-ride-on toy came from a university assignment to design a piece of children's luggage. Law's early designs won an award from the Princes Trust, but the business he subsequently started failed within two years.

Undeterred, Law decided to present his prototype on the BBC television programme *Dragons' Den* in 2006. Things didn't entirely go according to plan when one of the 'dragons' pulled on the strap of the sample Trunki and broke it. Another dragon described the product as 'worthless'. Since then, after a little more attention to quality control, the company has sold more than 1.3 million Trunki suitcases in 1,564 stores in 62 countries (as of June 2012). It is estimated that 10% of Britain's three-to six-year-olds now own a Trunki, and the company has developed an expanded range of products that includes a children's swimming backpack and a toy box that doubles as a ride, rocker and cart.

Lesson: If at first the wheels fall off, don't give up.

BRITISH MILITARY FITNESS (BMF)

The first ever BMF class in 1999 attracted just three clients. Since then more than 25,000 members have paid to be shouted at by a man in uniform while they're writhing around on the ground in exhaustion.

Founder Robin Cope, an ex-special forces major, set up British Military Fitness because he was unimpressed by what he saw as a gym culture which lacked proper motivation. His idea was to provide a way for people to join structured exercise classes outdoors in public parks across Britain. The classes are run by former or serving members of the British armed forces with recognised fitness-training qualifications – and loud voices. After gradually building up its clientele, the company began to expand with demand, although Cope has since admitted that they made the mistake of trying to 'grow too big too quickly' resulting in a debt of around £300,000. However one of the BMF class attendees was a City financier who agreed to invest a large sum in the company. This, along with a fair bit of positive press coverage, meant that by the mid-2000s, business was booming. And it still is, not unlike a sergeant major's voice.

Lesson: Don't try to yomp before you can march.

ASOS

In 2000 Nick Robertson, great-grandson of tailor Austin Reed, and former ad man Quentin Griffiths saw an opportunity to cash in on the wonderful world of celebrities (you may be familiar with the term 'the Kate effect'). So they founded the website ASOS (As Seen On Screen) as a portal for people to 'buy into' celebrity culture. Robertson explained: 'We read a stat back in 1999 that when the programme *Friends* aired, NBC got 4,000 calls about some standard lamp in one of their apartments asking where it could be purchased. So that was the real idea behind the business.' Initially the company wasn't intended as a global fashion online retailer, with the first ever sale being a pestle and mortar as seen on Jamie Oliver's *The Naked Chef*. Robertson stated that 'It wasn't until our first buyer came in, who was a fashion buyer, that we were pushed in that direction.' Annual revenue for 2012 was reported to be over £500 million and the company was described by *The Times* as 'the undisputed champion of online fashion'.

It now offers over 50,000 branded and own-label product lines across womenswear, menswear, footwear, accessories, jewellery and beauty, with approximately

1,500 new product lines being introduced each week.

Lesson: Never turn down the opportunity to become a dedicated follower of fashion.

TYRELLS CRISPS

Aged 24, William Chase took out a loan to buy his father's farm and for years followed the well-trodden but unprofitable path of selling 'attractive' but plain old potatoes until he had his road-to-Damascus moment (it may have been Swindon): start producing products that people would be prepared to pay a premium for.

So he borrowed an old fryer from a nearby fish and chip shop and tried his hand at making crisps. Happy with the results (and probably a lot heavier as a result of all the product testing he had to do himself), Chase took out a bank loan and founded Tyrells. Starting from scratch he took charge of everything, from production to PR. He also made the bold decision to sell his crisps exclusively to independent shops, and have them retail at premium prices: 'Reassuringly expensive', as Stella Artois would say.

Next came a classic story of David v Goliath; Chase discovered that supermarket giant Tesco was selling his products at discount prices, and this after he had expressly refused to sell to them. The media jumped on the spat, revelling in condemnations of 'bullying corporations'. Tesco hastily issued an apology and backed down, reaffirming their respect for 'small companies'.

Lesson: When your chips are down, try something new.

ELLA'S KITCHEN

After a career in accounting and a role as deputy managing director of children's TV channel Nickelodeon, founder Paul Lindley encapsulated all that he had learnt about children and marketing into the concept of Ella's Kitchen, named after his daughter whose eating habits had inspired him. He created a brand that appealed not only to 'mummies' (healthy and additive-free products) but to children as well by making the packaging fun and visually engaging. Curiously, fathers' preferences do not seem to have been taken into consideration.

Lindley managed to strike a revenue share deal with Nickelodeon to air adverts for his products, the first of which was 'the Red One' – as named by his son – an all-fruit smoothie. He also managed to secure a deal with Sainsbury's, who agreed to stock his products on a trial basis. That trial went on to become a full-scale deal, and Ella's Kitchen now has annual revenues of over £30 million. There is a lot to be said for children helping to pay for their school fees…

A top tip from the man himself: 'I made sure the cash flow in the business worked by having my customer pay me before I paid the supplier so I didn't have to bear the risk of cash tied up in stock'.

Lesson: Look close to home or even inside the home for inspiration.

BREWDOG

Both aged 24 (the optimal age to start a business?),

BrewDog co-founders James Watt and Martin Dickie were just not happy about the quality of lager available in the UK – presumably after a considerable amount of market research and product sampling. So they took out a bank loan to lease a building and buy some basic brewing equipment, selling the resulting beverage on the road and at local markets off the back of a van. Next they managed to secure further funding to buy the necessary equipment to expand. 'Tokyo', which claimed to be the UK's strongest-ever beer, was launched to massive media coverage. Meanwhile their other offering, Punk IPA, was heralded as 'the UK's fastest growing alternative beer brand'.

They used a creative way to fund the business, enabling people to buy shares in the company online, and resulting in over 1,300 thirsty investors (this is now commonly known as 'crowdfunding' and has become increasingly popular with start-ups looking for capital). They used that money to open the first BrewDog bar in Aberdeen, followed by 11 more craft beer bars across the country.

The company also benefited from the exposure of a media-hyped fallout with drinks giant Diageo and were named as the fastest-growing food and drink establishment in the UK by *The Sunday Times* in. Diageo must have found this accolade a touch bitter.

Lesson: People will be more inclined to buy your product if you brew up a storm of publicity.

BRAVISSIMO

Founder of lingerie brand Bravissimo, Sarah Tremellen

came up with her big idea on maternity leave when she struggled to find any attractive feel-good bras to fit her fuller bust. She realised that no one in the market was catering to the needs of D-L cup women, and that many of them were being offered 'enormous matronly contraptions more suitable for parachutes'. After taking an eight-week business course, Bravissimo was launched from her living room as a mail-order company. With the help of a friend, she created a catalogue and sent it out to a couple of hundred women, mostly friends and family.

Today, her customers are able to ask themselves 'which bra do I like?' rather than 'what comes in my size?' Over half a million women have become customers since the business began, turning it into a multimillion pound, award-winning lingerie, swimwear and nightwear company with 21 high street stores throughout Britain.

Lesson: Don't be shy about showing plenty of bra-vura when you get your big idea.

ST TROPEZ

Self-tanning product St Tropez is the invention of Californian couple Robyn and Tim Gibson, which beauty products wholesaler Judy Naaké single-handedly turned into a world-famous brand. When approached by the couple to act as European distributor of the then-unknown fake tan, London-based Naaké initially turned them down until learning that it contained aloe vera (which is apparently a good thing). Once Naaké tried it on, she instantly became a fan of the tan – persuading her bank manager to lend her £12,000 by rubbing the lotion onto the back of his hand. At the time she was selling St Tropez to salons and spas from her car boot. Before long she was rubbing it onto the legs of the editor of *Vogue*, but her biggest break came when Victoria Beckham was photographed by paparazzi carrying a transparent bag containing bottles of St. Tropez. (Was it for her or her husband? We may never know.) In 2006 she sold her business to venture capitalists LDC for £70m, and will forever be known as 'the world's fake tan queen.'

Lesson: Fake it till you make it.

There's no point in pretending that you know everything about running a business– nobody does – but if you've got this far and absorbed at least a modicum of the information and advice contained within these pages, then you will almost certainly know more than 99% of the rest of the human race does about what having your own business involves, why it can make a positive contribution to society, why it can enhance your social status and improve your lifestyle, why it can occupy your every waking thought, and how you can pretend to be better at it than you are.

What you now do with this information is up to you, but here's a suggestion: be confident about your new-found knowledge, see how far it takes you, but above all have fun using it. You are now a bona fide expert in the art of bluffing about how to be the next Google or Apple. And who knows, maybe you will. Just don't ever expect to achieve this overnight.

**Think you've got what it takes
to run your own business? Then take
our quiz at bluffers.com.**

GLOSSARY

I f you ever want to be a big business, you have to talk like a big business from the start.

Major companies don't 'do' things, they 'perform' (as in: 'The company has performed well this year'). They don't 'have' things, though they might 'enjoy' them ('We enjoyed a 50% increase in sales'). They are not 'run', they 'operate'. They are not 'helped by' anything, they 'benefit' from something. They don't 'buy' but they do 'acquire'. They don't 'make deals', they 'conduct transactions'. Their figures 'say' nothing but they may 'reflect' something. Their problems and opportunities are not 'seen' but 'identified'.

A number of expressions of this sort might prove useful when trying to camouflage the size (and condition) of your enterprise:

Unlimited opportunity for growth The business is now at rock bottom.

Room for improvement remains It can't get any worse.

Disappointing results Total disaster.

Predict Hope for.

Expect Wish for.

Anticipate Pray for.

Put assets to work Sell off assets to cover losses.

Prioritise Cut.

Selective purchasing Constant prioritising.

Prudent financial management Selective purchasing on a massive scale.

Rationalise Make excuses for.

Unique product Product no one else is brave enough to try to sell.

Temporary cash-flow crisis Time to jump out of a top-floor window.

Shortfall Long fall (usually by the finance director from a top-floor window – *see* above).

Market segmentation The process of dividing humanity into the nice people who might buy your product and the ungrateful scumbags who won't.

Cyclical market Why you are not to blame for the dramatic drop in sales.

Adverse market conditions Failed to sell anything.

Reactive marketing strategy Waiting to see what turns up.

Opportunistic marketing strategy Hoping something will turn up.

Keeping all our options open No strategy whatsoever.

Strategic A useful prefix that can be placed in front of almost any business expression to make it sound more impressive.

Improved performance Things didn't get noticeably worse.

Perceptible improvement One you might just see if you look hard enough in the right place.

Notable improvement One that you don't have to look too hard for.

Significant improvement One so apparent that even an investor might notice it without your having to point it out more than six or seven times.

Healthy profits Any profits at all, unless they exceed all expectations (*see* below).

Profits exceeded all our expectations You accidentally made a profit when your accountant told you not to for tax reasons.

Interim dividend A method of getting one's cash out of the business in a hurry.

Learning curve Why you have no idea what you are supposed to be doing.

Stable Stagnant.

Exciting opportunity Long shot.

Considerable boost Lucky break.

Long-term prospects The boss's favourite daydream.

Cautious but positive outlook The directors are stiff with Valium.

Redeployment Someone gets fired.

Restructuring Everyone gets fired.

Repositioning the business in the marketplace Looking for a completely different business to go into.

Diversifying Cutting one's losses in one's existing businesses.

Highly geared Heavily in debt.

Recapitalise for new development Get someone to extend your existing loans.

Expanding overseas operations Seeking some market, any market, that wants what you offer.

Subject to macroeconomic factors Totally out of control.

Slowdown in growth Dead stop and into reverse.

Economic downturn Business sinking fast.

Serious economic downturn Going under for the third time.

Severe economic downturn Glug, glug, glug.

Debtors Blood-sucking leeches who refuse to pay you.

Creditors Blood-sucking leeches who insist that you pay them.

Development plan What you would do if only you had the money.

Increase in cash terms Decrease in real terms.

Asset rich No cash.

Increased asset value You have a lot of unsold stock on your hands.

Tax purposes Ancient and mysterious incantation used by accountants when asked to justify their more illogical recommendations.

Interest Money taken away from you when you don't have any.

Income tax Money taken away from you when you eventually manage to make some at last.

Tax-deductible Reason given for the insistence that anything resembling a receipt is kept, no matter how small the amount, whether you need to or not (even if you're not yet paying tax).

Opportunity to liquidise previously committed assets House repossessed.

Favourable long-term outlook Horrifying short-term outlook.

The relevant statistic The one that puts the business in the best light.

The real issue The one that enables you to quote the relevant statistic.

Broad-based approach You haven't made up your mind yet.

Possible business contact Anyone you've ever heard of.

Good business contact Any possible business contact you've ever seen or spoken to, however briefly.

Networking Exploiting contacts ruthlessly.

Associate Good business contact who has been thoroughly networked.

Administration Paperwork.

Petty cash Contents of boss's pocket.

Company reserves Contents of boss's spouse's pocket.

Management accounts Back of the envelope in which one's bank statement came.

Finance director Expensive bookkeeper.

Administrative director The boss's PA.

Marketing, HR and R&D director The boss's spouse (on the payroll for tax purposes).

Customers Clients who insist on carrying something away in return for their money.

Clients Customers who are prepared to accept that you have given them something in return for their money without actually carrying it away.

Valued customer/client One whose cheque didn't bounce.

Congratulations. You are now fluent in business lingo.

BLUFFING NOTES

Bluffing Notes

Bluffing Notes

Bluffing Notes

Bluffing Notes

Bluffing Notes

Bluffing Notes

Bluffing Notes

Bluffing Notes

Bluffing Notes

Bluffing Notes

Bluffing Notes

Bluffing Notes